THE ELEMENTS

Copper

Richard Beatty

BENCHMARK BOOKS

MARSHALL CAVENDISH
NEW YORK

Benchmark Books
Marshall Cavendish Corporation
99 White Plains Road
Tarrytown, New York 10591

© Marshall Cavendish Corporation, 2001

Library of Congress Cataloging-in-Publication Data
Beatty, Richard.
Copper / Richard Beatty.
p.   cm. — (The elements)
Includes index.
Summary: Explores the history of the useful metal
copper and explains its chemistry, its uses, and
its importance in our lives.
ISBN 0-7614-0945-9 (lib. bdg.)
1. Copper—Juvenile literature. [1. Copper.] I. Title.
II. Elements (Benchmark Books)
QD181.C9 B43 2001
546'.652—dc21   99-054235 CIP AC

Printed in Hong Kong

Picture credits

Front cover: Rosenfeld Images Ltd./Science Photo Library.
Back cover: Werner Forman Archive.
Corbis (UK) Ltd.: 27; Farrell Grehan 30; José Manuel Sanchis Calvete i, 7 (left); Lester V. Bergman 22;
Paul Seheult 21.
Galaxy Picture Library: STScl 7 (right).
Image Bank: Franklin Wagner 26.
Leslie Garland Picture Library: Andrew Lambert 20; Ian T. Cartwright 16, 23; Leslie Garland 25.
Science Photo Library: G. Muller/Struers GMBH 6; R. Maisonneuve/Publiphoto Diffusion 24;
Rosenfeld Images Ltd. 4.
Still Pictures: Peter Frischmuth 18.
Tony Stone Images: Lester Lefkowitz 12; Paul Chesley 14.
Werner Forman Archive: 9; British Museum iii, 5; Dallas Museum of Art 10.

Series created by Brown Partworks Ltd.
Designed by wda

Contents

What is copper?

Stacks of copper bars, such as the ones pictured, are often processed into electrical cabling or water pipes.

Copper is a soft, orange-brown metal that has been used by humans for at least 7,000 years. In the ancient world, before the Iron Age, copper was mixed, or alloyed, with tin to make bronze. Bronze was then shaped into tools and weapons.

Today, both copper and its compounds have many uses. Its attractive color has always made it popular as a decorative metal, used for coinage and to make ornaments. Copper is an excellent conductor of electricity and heat, so it is chosen to make the flexible cables used in electrical wiring. Copper can be joined together easily and readily bent around corners, which makes it suitable to shape into pipes for heating systems. In small quantities it is also vital to insure the health of most animals and plants.

The copper atom

Everything you see around you is made up of tiny particles called atoms. Inside each atom are even smaller particles: protons, neutrons, and electrons. The protons and neutrons cluster together in the nucleus at the center of each atom. The electrons spin around the nucleus in a series of layers called electron shells.

Each copper atom has 29 negatively charged electrons. The number of electrons and protons is always the same, so copper has 29 positively charged protons in the nucleus. The number of protons also stands for the atomic number of an atom, so copper has an atomic number of 29.

Neutrons are about the same size as protons but have no electrical charge. One form, or isotope, of the copper atom has 34

COPPER ATOM

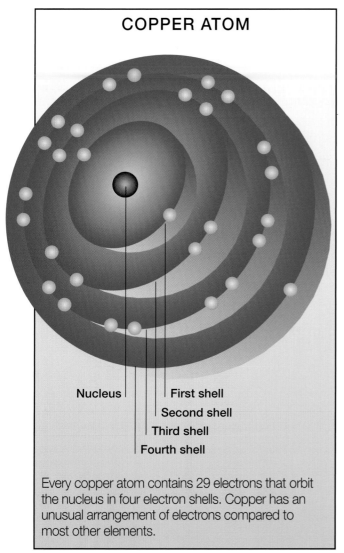

Nucleus
First shell
Second shell
Third shell
Fourth shell

Every copper atom contains 29 electrons that orbit the nucleus in four electron shells. Copper has an unusual arrangement of electrons compared to most other elements.

Copper and its chemistry

The chemistry of copper—how it combines with other atoms and molecules to form different substances—is decided by the behavior of its electrons. The electrons fill up electron shells from the center. As one shell fills, the electrons go into the next shell out. In most elements, the outermost shell is not complete. Only a full shell is stable, so elements share or exchange electrons to try and gain a complete outer shell. A copper atom will try and "lose" one or two of its electrons—the atom then has a positive charge and is called an ion.

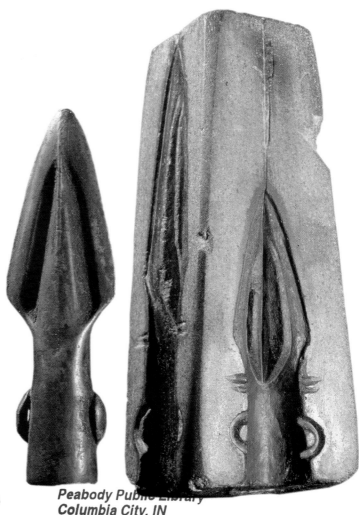

neutrons, while a second has 36 neutrons. Other isotopes also exist but they are radioactive, which means they usually break up into other elements. The isotopes of copper that contain 34 and 36 neutrons are called stable isotopes because they are not radioactive.

A bronze spear head and mold of Celtic origin.
Bronze is an alloy of copper and tin.

5

This is a magnified light micrograph image showing a thin section of metallic copper. Pure copper is made up of brightly colored, tiny crystals, or grains, which line up together in an ordered way.

Copper atoms arrange themselves in a densely packed pattern called a face-centered cubic structure. Unlike salt crystals, metal crystals are not brittle—the sheets of atoms that form them can slide past one another without coming apart. This is why most metals can be beaten into shape and drawn into a wire.

Atoms in metals lose their outer electrons, which float through the crystal structure as a "sea of electrons." The free electrons conduct heat and electricity. Copper is a particularly good conductor of both heat and electricity.

Most elements only try to lose the electrons in the outer shell. In transition metals, however, which include copper and iron, the last two electron shells are also involved, and their chemistry changes. The transition metals are usually heavy and often form colored compounds. They are important in industry.

Copper as a metal

Similar to other metals, copper is made up of tiny crystals too small to be seen by the eye. Each crystal, or grain, consists of many atoms packed in a certain way.

COPPER FACTS

● **Chemical symbol** Cu

● **Atomic number** 29

● **Relative atomic mass** 63.546. The relative atomic mass measures the average amount of matter in the atom and is effectively equal to the number of protons and neutrons, since electrons are so light. The figure is not a whole number because copper is a mixture of two isotopes.

● **Melting point** 1,981°F (1,083°C)

● **Boiling point** 4,653°F (2,567°C)

● **Density** 8.96. In other words, copper weighs 8.96 times more than the same volume of water.

Where copper is found

Copper is found throughout the universe. The metal exists in meteorites that reach Earth from space, for example. Like many other elements, copper is thought to have formed and then been scattered by the nuclear reactions that occur in exploding stars called supernovas.

Copper is also widespread on Earth in compounds called carbonates, chlorides, sulfides, and also the free metal. Copper forms part of manganese nodules, which are deposits of minerals found on many parts of the seafloor. These underwater deposits may become a crucial source of copper in the future when the reserves of the metal in Earth's crust are used up.

Copper in Earth's crust

The distribution of copper results from millions of years of activity on our planet. Molten rock, rising within the crust, releases superheated water that dissolves

DID YOU KNOW?

ROCKS, MINERALS, AND ORES
Rocks and minerals are not the same thing. A mineral is made up of certain chemical elements joined together in compounds. A rock is usually a mixture of several minerals. An ore is any rock that is a useful source of metal. Ores usually contain many ore minerals. During processing, useful minerals are separated from the rock, leaving waste products, or gangue. Although there are many different types of rock, only those used to produce metals are called ores.

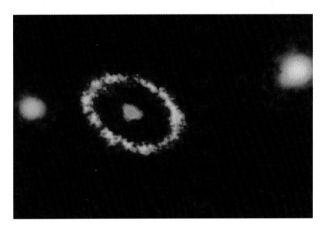

A yellow ring of debris, thought to contain copper, is the result of the nuclear reactions that occur in exploding stars called supernovas (seen here in red).

copper minerals and redeposits them within other rocks. Usually, copper combines with sulfur to form sulfide minerals. However, copper is not a very reactive element, and it is often found as the pure metal.

This picture shows a sample of the minerals quartz (SiO_2) and chalcopyrite ($CuFeS_2$).

When sulfide minerals are exposed to air or surface water, they slowly react with oxygen, turning into other minerals. Since they were nearer the surface and often colorful, these minerals were probably the first used by prehistoric people.

There are hundreds of different copper minerals, some of which are listed in the tables below. However, the most important source of copper is the sulfide mineral chalcopyrite ($CuFeS_2$), which is found in huge deposits, especially in the Americas.

COPPER FACTS			
Important sulfur-containing copper minerals			
Mineral name	*Chemical formula*	*Chemical name*	*Color of mineral*
Bornite	Cu_5FeS_4	a sulfide of both copper and iron	bronze colored, tarnishing to purplish brown
Chalcocite	Cu_2S	copper (I) sulfide	dark gray-brown
Chalcopyrite	$CuFeS_2$	copper-iron sulfide	shiny yellow
Covellite	CuS	copper (II) sulfide	blue-black

COPPER FACTS			
Important oxygen-containing copper minerals			
Mineral name	*Chemical formula*	*Chemical name*	*Color of mineral*
Azurite	$2CuCO_3.Cu(OH)_2$	copper carbonate with copper hydroxide	blue
Chrysocolla	$CuSiO_3.2H_2O$	copper silicate dihydrate	bluish-green (variable)
Cuprite	Cu_2O	copper (I) oxide	reddish brown
Malachite	$CuCO_3.Cu(OH)_2$	copper carbonate with copper hydroxide	green
Tenorite	CuO	copper (II) oxide	black

The history of copper

The importance of copper to human society dates back to prehistoric times. Even before humans had developed techniques to free metals from their ores, pure copper was found in Earth's crust and was available for people to make ornaments and tools. Colorful copper ores, too, were often used as pigments.

Metalworking in the Old World

The earliest evidence for copper working, dating back around 10,000 years (to 8000 B.C.E.), comes from western Asia (the Near East). Somewhat later, before 5000 B.C.E., people in the same region began to use heat to smelt (separate) copper from its

This sculpture from the mastaba (tomb) of a fifth dynasty (c. 2494–2345 B.C.E.) Egyptian pharaoh shows Egyptian metalworkers at a forge.

Thousands of years ago, the Romans set up large copper mines on Cyprus, an island in the Mediterranean Sea. The name *copper* comes from the Latin word *cuprum,* which means "metal of Cyprus." The chemical symbol for copper, Cu, also comes from this Latin word.

ores. Heat was also used to melt the copper and cast it into useful shapes. Some copper ores naturally contain the element arsenic. This element added hardness to the metal, making it better for tools and weapons.

Sometime before 3500 B.C.E., bronze—an alloy of copper and tin—was developed and the so-called "Bronze Age" of Europe and Asia began. Bronze played an ever-increasing role in society. A major new weapon, the sword, was made from bronze. Metalworking techniques became more and more complex. Many are recorded in great detail in the tomb paintings of ancient Egypt.

The development of iron around 1000 B.C.E. meant that bronze lost its appeal as a weapon-making material. However,

This picture shows part of a ceremonial headdress from Colombia, dating from 1000–1600 C.E. It is made from an alloy of copper and gold.

bronze was still used for decoration and certain other purposes, particularly in ancient China where metalworking techniques became highly sophisticated. Brass—an alloy of copper and zinc—was also introduced soon after the Iron Age.

The Americas

In North America, copper working probably developed around the huge deposits of pure metal that existed in the

regions surrounding the Great Lakes. However, true metallurgy probably began in South America (in what are now Peru and Ecuador), where copper may have been smelted before 1000 B.C.E.

South and Central American civilizations created many alloys of copper by carefully mixing the metal with gold and silver. These were often used to make religious objects and were valued for their bright colors. By the time of the European invasions in the 16th century, bronze had also been developed by the Incas of Peru.

Later history

In medieval Europe, brass became more widely used than bronze for many purposes. It was also used for another new weapon—the cannon.

With the advent of the scientific and industrial revolutions, copper alloys— especially brass—became increasingly important in everyday life. They were used for precision instruments, domestic utensils, engine components, and for coinage.

The use of metallic copper made a comeback from the 1880s, when scientists

German artist Ferdinand Knab completed this impression of the Colossus of Rhodes in 1886. It belongs to the Museum of Art and History in Berlin, Germany.

began to learn about electricity. Copper is an extremely ductile metal, which means it can be drawn into long wires—especially suitable for electrical wiring. At around the same time, copper sulfate began to be sprayed on plant crops to control disease. In the 20th century, many new uses were developed for copper and its compounds.

DID YOU KNOW?

THE COLOSSUS OF RHODES
The Colossus of Rhodes was a huge bronze statue constructed in 250 B.C.E. for the Greek sun god Helios. It was one of the Seven Wonders of the World. It stood at the entrance to the harbor on the Greek island of Rhodes and was about 100 ft (30 m) high. Destroyed by an earthquake around 225 B.C.E., the statue lay in ruins underwater for nearly a thousand years. Eventually, the metal was collected and sold as scrap—an early example of recycling metal.

From ore to metal

Extracting, or refining, copper from its ore is a huge worldwide industry. About 90 percent of Earth's copper reserves are found in just four locations: the great basin of the western United States, central Canada, the Andes region of Peru and Chile, and Zambia in Africa. In each case, the copper industry is vitally important to the region's economy.

Mining

Modern mining is a highly mechanized process. The largest mines, such as those of the United States, are open-pit mines, dug out into a series of terraces. Large holes are drilled in the ore, the holes are filled with explosives, and the rock is then blasted loose. Once enough material is gathered, the copper ore is scooped up by huge diggers, loaded into dumpster trucks, and taken to a copper refinery.

This picture shows a copper mine in New Mexico in the United States. Over 90 percent of the world's copper is excavated from mines such as this one.

Concentrating the ore

Most copper ores contain only about 1 percent metal, so the ore must be concentrated in a process called flotation. This is done by first pulverizing the ore, mixing it with water, and then passing it through a series of large water-filled tanks containing foam-producing chemicals. Copper-containing minerals are trapped in the foam at the surface of the tank and scooped off, while the unwanted material, or gangue, sinks to the bottom.

The end result is a concentrate containing about 25 to 35 percent copper by weight. This is dried and sent for smelting. The concentrated ore may also contain other valuable metals, such as silver, which are recovered later.

Smelting and refining

Smelting uses the very high temperatures inside furnaces to remove most of the impurities from the concentrated ore. The details are complicated and different for each copper-containing mineral. The easiest ores to smelt are the copper oxides, but the most commonly mined copper minerals—copper sulfides—present greater difficulties. Here, copper is removed from its ore by heating it with oxygen gas (O_2). At the same time, the sulfur in the copper sulfide ores is oxidized to sulfur dioxide gas (SO_2). Since sulfur dioxide is a major contributor to acid rain, many modern copper refineries collect the gas and process it into sulfuric acid (H_2SO_4).

The product of this smelting—an impure metal called blister copper—goes through two refining stages called fire refining and electrorefining. Electrorefining is the last stage and yields copper that is about 99.99 percent pure.

Electrorefining involves a chemical process called electrolysis, which uses electricity to purify the blister copper. An electric current is applied to two copper plates immersed in a tank of copper sulfate ($CuSO_4$) solution. One of the plates, called the cathode, is made of pure copper. This plate is connected to the negative terminal of the electricity source. Copper ions in the solution are attracted to this plate and deposit onto it as pure copper.

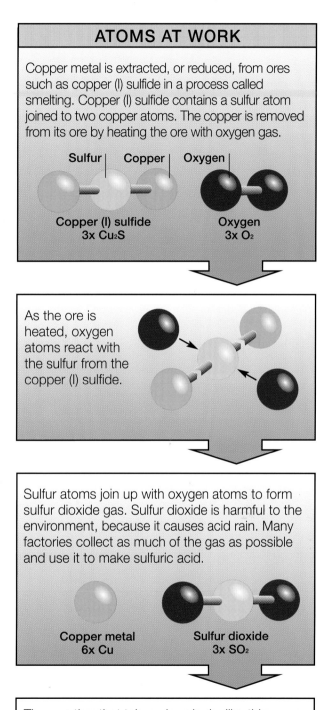

ATOMS AT WORK

Copper metal is extracted, or reduced, from ores such as copper (I) sulfide in a process called smelting. Copper (I) sulfide contains a sulfur atom joined to two copper atoms. The copper is removed from its ore by heating the ore with oxygen gas.

Sulfur | Copper | Oxygen |

Copper (I) sulfide
3x Cu_2S

Oxygen
3x O_2

As the ore is heated, oxygen atoms react with the sulfur from the copper (I) sulfide.

Sulfur atoms join up with oxygen atoms to form sulfur dioxide gas. Sulfur dioxide is harmful to the environment, because it causes acid rain. Many factories collect as much of the gas as possible and use it to make sulfuric acid.

Copper metal
6x Cu

Sulfur dioxide
3x SO_2

The reaction that takes place looks like this:

$$3Cu_2S + 3O_2 \rightarrow 6Cu + 3SO_2$$

This shows that three molecules of copper (I) sulfide react with three molecules of oxygen to give six atoms of copper and three molecules of sulfur dioxide.

The other plate, called the anode, is made of the impure blister copper. This plate is connected to the positively charged terminal. Electricity makes copper from the anode dissolve into the copper sulfate solution and move toward the cathode. Several rare metals, such as gold and silver, are often found in copper ores, and they are also recovered during electrolysis.

Hydrometallurgy

Hydrometallurgy is the name give to extraction using water and other liquids. Much of hydrometallurgy is concerned with leaching—obtaining metals by dissolving them from rocks. Leaching becomes useful when there is not enough copper in the rock to smelt economically.

The extremely high temperatures used to smelt copper from its ores mean that workers have to wear protective clothing.

Leaching is usually done at the surface of the copper mine, either on freshly mined ore or from waste dumps that still contain copper. Generally, it is easier to leach oxide ores than sulfide ores.

Once the copper is leached from its ore, it must be retrieved from the solution. Most modern copper refineries use a technique called solvent extraction. Here, dissolved copper is transferred to a non-watery liquid called a solvent and then redissolved in water in a purer form. The metal is then obtained by electrowinning, a method very similar to electrorefining.

ATOMS AT WORK

Bright blue crystals of copper sulfate are one of the best-known and most important copper compounds. They can be made by adding sulfuric acid to black copper (II) oxide powder.

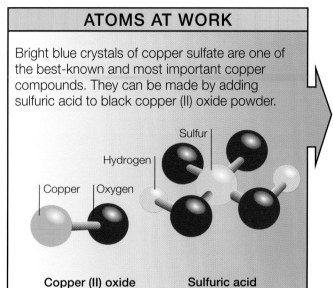

Sulfur

Hydrogen

Copper | Oxygen

Copper (II) oxide
CuO

Sulfuric acid
H_2SO_4

When sulfuric acid is added to water the bonds between the hydrogen atoms and the oxygen atoms break, and the acid splits into hydrogen ions and sulfate ions. When acids are added to water they are known as dilute acids.

Hydrogen ions
2x H^+

Sulfate ion
SO_4^{2-}

Chemistry and compounds

A characteristic of many metals is that their compounds can be brightly colored, usually quite unlike the color of the metals in their native (pure) state. Copper compounds are no exception to the rule. Indeed, copper forms several colored compounds with other elements. For example, copper (II) oxide (CuO) is black, copper carbonate ($CuCO_3$) is green, and copper sulfate ($CuSO_4$) and copper nitrate ($Cu[NO_3]_2$) are blue. Copper (I) sulfide (Cu_2S) ranges from black (in its purest form) to dull yellow, depending on how impure the sample is. Many of these compounds are a familiar part of the high-school chemistry laboratory. They are also extremely important in industry.

When copper (II) oxide is added to the dilute sulfuric acid, the atoms are exchanged. The hydrogen ions attach to the oxygen atom to make water. A copper atom joins with a sulfate ion to give copper sulfate

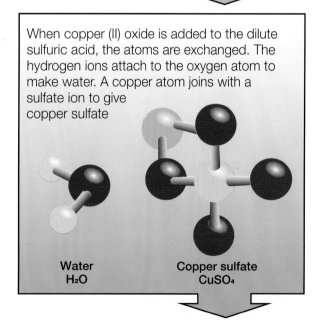

Water
H_2O

Copper sulfate
$CuSO_4$

The reaction between copper (II) oxide and dilute sulfuric acid looks like this:

$$CuO + H_2SO_4 \rightarrow CuSO_4 + H_2O$$

This equation tells us that one molecule of copper (II) oxide reacts with one molecule of sulfuric acid to give one molecule of copper sulfate and one molecule of water.

Chemistry of copper

Copper is not particularly reactive compared to most other metals. It is very resistant to attack by oxygen and water: copper only changes to copper (II) oxide (CuO) at a temperature of 570°F (300°C). It is not corroded by water, or even steam, which is why it is so useful as piping for heating and water systems. This hardy metal does not even react with dilute acids, such as hydrochloric acid (HCl) or sulfuric acid (H_2SO_4), although

Fishing boats are often coated with copper-based antifouling paint to help protect the wooden hull against attack by microorganisms that live in the sea.

concentrated nitric acid (HNO_3) reacts violently with the metal. It also reacts slowly with gases in the air.

Like other elements, copper forms chemical bonds with other elements in two main ways. It may share some of its electrons with another atom, forming what is known as a covalent bond. Alternatively, it can "lose" one or two electrons entirely and become a positively charged copper ion.

The lost electrons are transferred to the atom of another element, which then becomes negatively charged. The two atoms are held together by electrical attraction. This kind of bond is called an ionic, or electrovalent, bond.

Copper ions

Most metal atoms lose electrons when they form ionic bonds, because the resulting metal ion often has a more stable electronic structure. Copper forms two main ions. When copper loses one of its electrons, the copper ion is written as Cu^+. When it loses two electrons the copper ion is written as Cu^{2+}. This ion, Cu^{2+}, is more stable when dissolved in water.

In compounds, Cu^+ normally shows a valency (combining power) of 1, whereas Cu^{2+} has a valency of 2. For example, copper can combine with oxygen in two different ways. When copper loses one of its electrons to an oxygen atom, forming

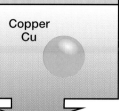

ATOMS AT WORK

Copper, brass, bronze, and other objects made with copper often corrode if they are left outside.

Copper Cu

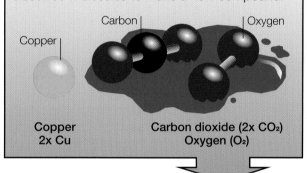

Air contains carbon and oxygen atoms held together as carbon dioxide molecules. It also contains oxygen atoms held together as pairs in molecules. All these molecules dissolve in water if the air is moist. Copper atoms will react with the dissolved molecules to make a new compound.

Copper | | Carbon | | Oxygen

Copper 2x Cu | **Carbon dioxide (2x CO_2) Oxygen (O_2)**

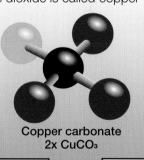

The compound that forms when copper reacts with oxygen and carbon dioxide is called copper carbonate. Copper carbonate is an attractive green color. It forms a coating over the copper object and protects the object from further corrosion.

Copper carbonate 2x $CuCO_3$

The reaction between copper, oxygen, and carbon dioxide is written like this:

$2Cu + 2CO_2 + O_2 \rightarrow 2CuCO_3$

This tells us that two atoms of copper, two molecules of carbon dioxide, and one molecule of oxygen react to give two molecules of copper carbonate.

the Cu^+ ion, the compound has the formula Cu_2O and is commonly called copper (I) oxide or cuprous oxide. When copper loses two electrons to the oxygen atom it forms the Cu^{2+} ion. The resulting compound has the formula CuO and is called copper (II) oxide or cupric oxide.

Using copper compounds

Copper compounds are often used mainly for the copper ions they contain. For this

A farmer sprays a solution of copper sulfate onto a plantation of fruit trees. Plants may suffer from poor growth and become much more prone to disease if the soil in which they grow lacks copper.

reason, several different compounds may be useful for the same task.

For example, copper ions are very poisonous to most microorganisms, algae, and fungi, but not to animals or higher plants. As a result, various salts of copper are used to protect wood against rot, to dust seeds and plants against fungal attack, and to prevent green scum growing in swimming pools. They are also used widely in agriculture to guard against copper deficiency.

Copper sulfate ($CuSO_4$) is the compound produced in the greatest amounts. This compound is the main starting point used to make other copper chemicals in the inorganic chemical industry. It is also the main copper-based fertilizer used in agriculture. Since copper sulfate dissolves in water, the compound can be applied to the soil or to the leaves of growing plants as a spray.

Copper sulfate has traditionally been used to make a fungicide called Bordeaux mixture, which was once used to spray the vineyards of the famous wine-growing region called Bordeaux in France. Seeds are also dipped in copper sulfate solution to prevent disease.

Plants are able to benefit from a spray of copper, but numerous pests are not. Consequently, many farmers use copper salts, such as copper nitrate ($Cu[NO_3]_2$) and copper sulfate, to poison fungi and molds that destroy their crops.

Examples of other useful compounds include copper (I) oxide (Cu_2O), which is

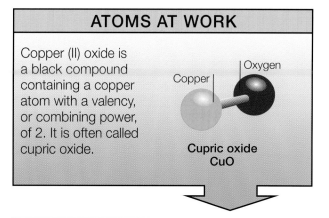

ATOMS AT WORK

Copper (II) oxide is a black compound containing a copper atom with a valency, or combining power, of 2. It is often called cupric oxide.

Oxygen
Copper

Cupric oxide
CuO

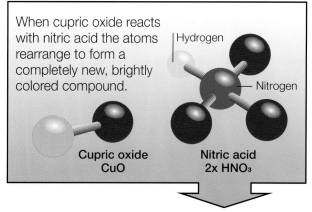

When cupric oxide reacts with nitric acid the atoms rearrange to form a completely new, brightly colored compound.

Hydrogen

Nitrogen

Cupric oxide
CuO

Nitric acid
2x HNO₃

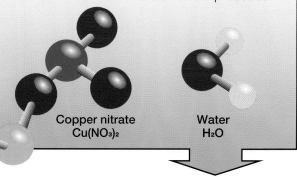

The new compound that forms is called copper nitrate, which appears as blue crystals during the reaction. A molecule of water is also produced.

Copper nitrate
Cu(NO₃)₂

Water
H₂O

The reaction that takes place when cupric oxide reacts with nitric acid is written like this:

$$CuO + 2HNO_3 \rightarrow Cu(NO_3)_2 + H_2O$$

The number of atoms of each element is the same on both sides of the equation, although the atoms have joined up in new combinations.

used as a fungicide in antifouling paints to protect wood and other surfaces against attack by fungi, and copper (II) chloride ($CuCl_2$), used to remove foul-smelling sulfur compounds from oil.

Colors and complexes

Compounds that contain the Cu^{2+} ion are widely used for coloring glass, pottery, and textiles. The behavior of the electrons in each of the copper atoms determines the color of the copper compound.

A Cu^{2+} ion has lost one of the electrons from its third electron shell. This electron shell is actually made up of three subshells. One subshell is called the d subshell. It usually contains ten electrons, but with the Cu^{2+} ion it only contains nine. In addition, the d subshell is made of five different orbitals that

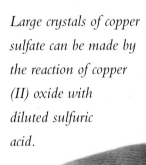

Large crystals of copper sulfate can be made by the reaction of copper (II) oxide with diluted sulfuric acid.

point in different directions, with room for two electrons in each orbital.

Orbitals have a certain amount of energy. When the Cu^{2+} ion is on its own, each orbital has the same energy. However, the Cu^{2+} ion often forms complexes with molecules such as water or ammonia. With copper complexes, these molecules arrange themselves around the Cu^{2+} ion in an ordered way. The molecules also change the energy of each orbital in the d subshell. The Cu^{2+} ion contains one free orbital. An electron from an orbital with low energy can jump into the free orbital. As it jumps, the electron absorbs light of a certain color. This makes the copper complex look colored.

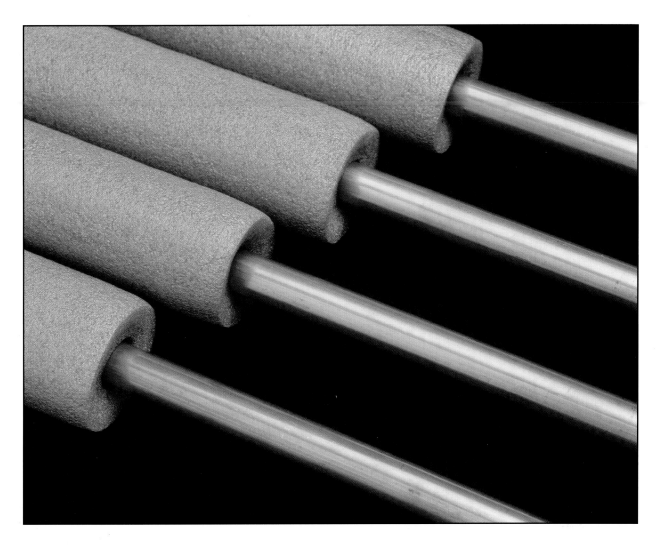

Using the metal

Copper is a good heat conductor, so water pipes are often insulated with foam to stop the heat escaping.

Most pure metals are mixed, or alloyed, with other elements before they are used. Copper forms alloys more easily than most other metals. Each element added to the alloy gives the alloy special properties. Some make the alloy stronger; others change its color, give it greater tensile strength, or make it resistant to corrosion or wear.

Pure copper also has many applications. Every year, about 4 million tons (3.6 million tonnes) of copper are used to make electrical wiring. Copper is also used to make water and gas pipes in homes. Due to the softness of the metal, copper pipes are relatively easy to bend into shape. Copper is also poisonous to bacteria, so the pipes help to insure a safe water supply.

In construction, copper is often used to protect the roofs of public buildings. Copper gradually corrodes if it is left outdoors. As well as protecting the copper from further corrosion, the layer of copper carbonate ($CuCO_3$) that develops on its surface is valued as decoration.

Copper alloys

Copper alloys are used for countless products, from scientific instruments to engine parts. The most important copper alloys are brass, bronze, aluminum bronze, and copper–nickel alloy.

Brass is an alloy of copper and zinc, and it was once one of the most widely used copper alloys. By the 19th century, brass was used to make corrosion-resistant decorative brasswork, such as door knockers and jewelry. The development of plastics and steel during the 20th century, however, has reduced the demand for brass objects. Today, brass is still valued for its decorative qualities. For example, certain musical instruments, such as the trumpet and trombone, are made from brass because the alloy is light, strong, and easy to shape. Many coins are still made of brass.

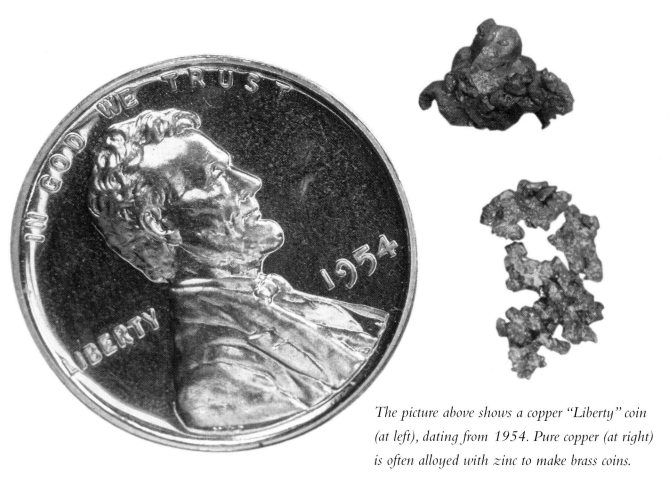

The picture above shows a copper "Liberty" coin (at left), dating from 1954. Pure copper (at right) is often alloyed with zinc to make brass coins.

Bronze is an alloy of copper and tin made from nine parts copper to one part tin. Before the discovery of iron, bronze was the main material used to make tools and weapons. Statues are often made from an alloy of copper, tin, and lead. Lead helps the molten alloy flow better. Phosphor bronze is an alloy of copper, tin, and the element phosphorus. It is very strong and resistant to corrosion, so it is often used in the moving parts of heavy machinery.

Aluminum bronze is a 20th-century development. As its name suggests, aluminum bronze is an alloy of copper and a small amount of the metal aluminum. Ships' propellers are often made from aluminum bronze. Aluminum adds the properties of strength and resistance to corrosion to the alloy.

Nickel and copper make an alloy that forms a range of useful materials with an exceptional resistance to corrosion. Copper-nickel alloys are used in the construction of offshore oil rigs, for example. Nickel silver, or German silver, is the name for a series of alloys of copper, nickel, and zinc. The name comes from the silvery appearance of products made from the alloy, such as coinage and tableware.

This picture shows a ship's propeller cast from an alloy of aluminum and copper.

One ancient method, used to produce very detailed castings, is called the "lost-wax" method. An original model is made in wax and then covered in layers of clay. The clay-covered wax model is then heated to remove the wax, leaving behind a clay mold. A molten alloy, such as bronze, is then poured into the mold and allowed to cool. The mold is then broken open to reveal the bronze casting. Larger castings, such as ships' propellers, are made using molds shaped from sand and cement. Many tons of metal are used, and the propeller can take days to complete.

Copper can also be shaped by hammering or pressing. To make copper tubing, for example, a solid cylinder of copper is heated and placed in a powerful

Copper forms many other alloys when mixed with other elements. For example, it is often alloyed with gold and silver to make attractive jewelry. Copper forms an exceptionally strong alloy with the metal beryllium. However, beryllium is extremely poisonous, and the alloy has to be made under careful conditions.

Shaping and forming

Copper and copper alloys can be shaped using many different metalworking techniques. In casting, for example, the metal is melted and then poured into a mold, where it cools and solidifies.

Sheets of welded copper are rolled for storage at a foundry. Nearly half of all pure copper manufactured from its ore is used to make flexible electrical wiring.

24

Molten bronze is removed from a furnace at a bell foundry in Jura, France. The molten bronze is poured into a mold and allowed to solidify. The mold is then removed, and the bell is filed to shape and tuned.

hydraulic ram. The ram squeezes the copper around the outside of a circular obstruction. Once the copper has cooled, the obstruction is removed, revealing the copper tube inside.

Different equipment is used to produce a variety of shapes. Rolling mills turn copper into thin sheets. Strands of copper can also be pulled through the hole of a shaping tool called a die. Each die squeezes the copper into fine strands. This method is used to produce copper wiring.

Copper in biology

In small amounts, copper is vital to most plants and animals. Essential parts of the body chemistry of many organisms would stop working without it.

What copper does

Copper is particularly important in helping organisms to use oxygen from the air.

In humans and other vertebrates (animals with backbones), oxygen is transported from the lungs to the tissues by a chemical called hemoglobin, which is found in red blood cells. Hemoglobin is a protein that contains iron in its structure. Without copper, however, the body cannot make hemoglobin in the first place.

Other creatures, including lobsters, snails, and spiders, use a different oxygen-carrying protein—called hemocyanin—that does contain copper. Hemocyanin works by binding a molecule of oxygen between two copper atoms. It gives the blood of these animals a bluish tinge.

Snails breathe by using a protein in their blood called hemocyanin. Hemocyanin contains two copper atoms that bind with oxygen taken from the air.

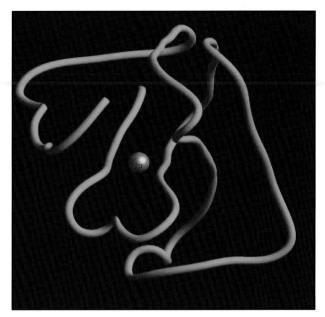

A three-dimensional computer-generated image shows a basic protein found in cucumbers. The twisted green ribbon is an amino acid string, and the orange sphere is a copper atom. Plants need copper to photosynthesize, that is, produce food using light.

Copper is also found in many proteins called enzymes, which are used to catalyze (speed up) biological reactions. For example, the final stage in the breakdown of food molecules within the body's cells depends on a copper-containing enzyme called cytochrome oxidase. This enzyme first binds an oxygen molecule between atoms of copper and iron. Oxygen then reacts with electrons and hydrogen ions from the breakdown of food, providing vital energy for the cell.

Copper-containing enzymes also have other roles, such as helping to make the tough protein fibers that bind the body together. In most plants, copper is needed for photosynthesis (producing food using light energy from the Sun).

The use of copper is thought to have started relatively late in evolution, perhaps after oxygen became plentiful in the atmosphere. The simplest organisms, such as bacteria and algae, do not use copper—in fact, it poisons them.

Diet and deficiency

On average, humans need around 2 mg (milligrams) of copper each day—a very small amount. Copper deficiency in people is uncommon, although it can be caused by rare diseases.

Farm animals sometimes suffer from copper deficiency if there is not enough copper in the soil. Lambs can be born with a disease called swayback, in which the hind legs do not work properly. Copper can be added to their food or to the soil to cure this condition.

Periodic table

Everything in the universe is made from combinations of substances called elements. Elements are the building blocks of matter. They are made of tiny atoms, which are much too small to see.

The character of an atom depends on how many even tinier particles called protons there are in its center, or nucleus. An element's atomic number is the same as the number of protons.

Scientists have found around 110 different elements. About 90 elements occur naturally on Earth. The rest have been made in experiments.

All these elements are set out on a chart called the periodic table. This lists all the elements in order according to their atomic number.

The elements at the left of the table are metals. Those at the right are nonmetals. Between the metals and the nonmetals are the metalloids, which sometimes act like metals and sometimes like nonmetals.

- On the left of the table are the alkali metals. These elements have just one electron in their outer shells.

- Elements get more reactive as you go down a group.

- On the right of the periodic table are the noble gases. These elements have full outer shells.

- The number of electrons orbiting the nucleus increases down each group.

- Elements in the same group have the same number of electrons in their outer shells.

- The transition metals are in the middle of the table, between Groups II and III.

Group I

| 1 H Hydrogen 1 |
| 3 Li Lithium 7 |
| 11 Na Sodium 23 |

Group II

| 4 Be Beryllium 9 |
| 12 Mg Magnesium 24 |

Transition metals

19 K Potassium 39	20 Ca Calcium 40	21 Sc Scandium 45	22 Ti Titanium 48	23 V Vanadium 51	24 Cr Chromium 52	25 Mn Manganese 55	26 Fe Iron 56	27 Co Cobalt 59
37 Rb Rubidium 85	38 Sr Strontium 88	39 Y Yttrium 89	40 Zr Zirconium 91	41 Nb Niobium 93	42 Mo Molybdenum 96	43 Tc Technetium (98)	44 Ru Ruthenium 101	45 Rh Rhodium 103
55 Cs Cesium 133	56 Ba Barium 137	71 Lu Lutetium 175	72 Hf Hafnium 179	73 Ta Tantalum 181	74 W Tungsten 184	75 Re Rhenium 186	76 Os Osmium 190	77 Ir Iridium 192
87 Fr Francium 223	88 Ra Radium 226	103 Lr Lawrencium (260)	104 Unq Unnilquadium (261)	105 Unp Unnilpentium (262)	106 Unh Unnilhexium (263)	107 Uns Unnilseptium (?)	108 Uno Unniloctium (?)	109 Une Unnilenium (?)

Lanthanide elements

| 57 La Lanthanum 39 | 58 Ce Cerium 140 | 59 Pr Praseodymium 141 | 60 Nd Neodymium 144 | 61 Pm Promethium (145) |

Actinide elements

| 89 Ac Actinium 227 | 90 Th Thorium 232 | 91 Pa Protactinium 231 | 92 U Uranium 238 | 93 Np Neptunium (237) |

The horizontal rows are called periods. As you go across a period, the atomic number increases by one from each element to the next. The vertical columns are called groups. Elements get heavier as you go down a group. All the elements in a group have the same number of electrons in their outer shells. This means they react in similar ways.

The transition metals fall between Groups II and III. Their electron shells fill up in an unusual way. The lanthanide elements and the actinide elements are set apart from the main table to make it easier to read. All the lanthanide elements and the actinide elements are quite rare.

Copper in the table

Copper has atomic number 29, so it has 29 protons in its nucleus. It is positioned in the middle of the table among the group of metals known as the transition metals.

Like many other metals, copper is shiny and a good conductor of electricity and heat. Like most other transition metals, copper's compounds tend to be colored.

Group VIII

Metals							2 He Helium 4
Metalloids (semimetals)		**Group III**	**Group IV**	**Group V**	**Group VI**	**Group VII**	
Nonmetals		5 B Boron 11	6 C Carbon 12	7 N Nitrogen 14	8 O Oxygen 16	9 F Fluorine 19	10 Ne Neon 20

29
Cu — Atomic (proton) number
Copper — Symbol / Name
64 — Atomic mass

			13 Al Aluminum 27	14 Si Silicon 28	15 P Phosphorus 31	16 S Sulfur 32	17 Cl Chlorine 35	18 Ar Argon 40
28 Ni Nickel 59	29 Cu Copper 64	30 Zn Zinc 65	31 Ga Gallium 70	32 Ge Germanium 73	33 As Arsenic 75	34 Se Selenium 79	35 Br Bromine 80	36 Kr Krypton 84
46 Pd Palladium 106	47 Ag Silver 108	48 Cd Cadmium 112	49 In Indium 115	50 Sn Tin 119	51 Sb Antimony 122	52 Te Tellurium 128	53 I Iodine 127	54 Xe Xenon 131
78 Pt Platinum 195	79 Au Gold 197	80 Hg Mercury 201	81 Tl Thallium 204	82 Pb Lead 207	83 Bi Bismuth 209	84 Po Polonium (209)	85 At Astatine (210)	86 Rn Radon (222)

62 Sm Samarium 150	63 Eu Europium 152	64 Gd Gadolinium 157	65 Tb Terbium 159	66 Dy Dysprosium 163	67 Ho Holmium 165	68 Er Erbium 167	69 Tm Thulium 169	70 Yb Ytterbium 173
94 Pu Plutonium (244)	95 Am Americium (243)	96 Cm Curium (247)	97 Bk Berkelium (247)	98 Cf Californium (251)	99 Es Einsteinium (252)	100 Fm Fermium (257)	101 Md Mendelevium (258)	102 No Nobelium (259)

Chemical reactions

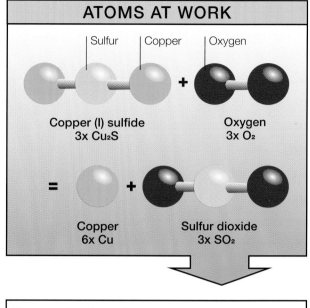

ATOMS AT WORK

Sulfur | Copper | Oxygen

Copper (I) sulfide
3x Cu_2S

Oxygen
3x O_2

=

Copper
6x Cu

Sulfur dioxide
3x SO_2

Chemical reactions are going on all the time—candles burn, nails rust, food is digested. Some reactions involve just two substances; others many more. But whenever a reaction takes place, at least one substance is changed.

In a chemical reaction, the atoms stay the same. But they join up in different combinations to form new molecules.

Writing an equation

Chemical reactions can be described by writing down the atoms and molecules before and the atoms and molecules after. Since the atoms stay the same, the number of atoms before will be the same

The reaction that takes place when copper is removed from copper (I) sulfide looks like this:

$$3Cu_2S + 3O_2 \rightarrow 6Cu + 3SO_2$$

This shows that three molecules of copper (I) sulfide react with three molecules of oxygen to give six atoms of copper and three molecules of sulfur dioxide.

as the number of atoms after. Chemists write the reaction as an equation. The equation shows what happens in the chemical reaction.

When the numbers of each atom on both sides of the equation are equal, the equation is balanced. If the numbers are not equal, something is wrong. So the chemist adjusts the number of atoms involved until the equation balances.

A copper ore is heated to melting point in preparation for copper extraction at a copper smelting plant in Antwerp, Belgium.

Glossary

alloy: A mixture of a metal with one or more other elements.

atom: The smallest part of an element that has all the properties of that element.

atomic number: The number of protons in an atom.

bond: The attraction between two atoms that holds them together.

catalyst: Something that makes a chemical reaction occur more quickly.

compound: A substance that is made of atoms of more than one element. The atoms in a molecule are held together by chemical bonds.

corrosion: The eating away of a material by reaction with other chemicals, often oxygen and moisture in the air.

electrolysis: The use of electricity to change a substance chemically.

electron: A tiny particle with a negative charge. Electrons are found inside atoms, where they move around the nucleus in layers called electron shells.

gangue: The worthless material in which valuable metals or minerals occur.

hydrometallurgy: The extraction of elements, such as metals, from their ores using water and other liquids.

ion: A particle of an element similar to an atom but carrying an additional negative or positive electrical charge.

isotopes: Atoms of an element with the same number of protons and electrons but different numbers of neutrons.

metal: An element on the left-hand side of the periodic table.

neutron: A tiny particle with no electrical charge. It is found in the nucleus of every atom.

nonmetal: An element on the right-hand side of the periodic table.

nucleus: The center of an atom. It contains protons and neutrons.

ore: A collection of minerals from which metals, in particular, are usually extracted.

oxidation: A reaction where oxygen is added, or one or more electrons are removed, from a substance.

periodic table: A chart of all the chemical elements laid out in order of their atomic number.

proton: A tiny particle with a positive charge. Protons are found inside the nucleus of an atom.

refining: An industrial process that frees elements, such as metals, from impurities or unwanted material.

solvent: A liquid that can dissolve or disperse one or more other substances.

tensile strength: The property of a substance that makes it resistant to the forces of stress.

transition metals: The group of metals that form a block in the middle of the periodic table.

Index